SUCCESS!

THE SECRET TO BECOMING HAPPY, HEALTHY, AND WEALTHY!

Christopher Mitchell

www.FitChristopherMitchell.com

SUCCESS! THE SECRET TO BECOMING HAPPY, HEALTHY, AND WEALTHY!

Copyright © 2017 Christopher Mitchell

ISBN-13: 978-1545282403

ISBN-10: 1545282404

Unless otherwise noted, all scriptures quoted are from the New International Version (NIV) of The Holy Bible. Copyright 1973, 1978, 1984, 2011 by Biblica, Inc. Used by permission. All rights reserved worldwide.

All rights reserved. Under International Copyright Law no part of this publication may be reproduced, stored in a retrieval system or transmitted in any form- digital, electronic, mechanical, photocopy, recording or any other form without the prior written permission of the author or publisher.

Printed In The United States Of America.

TABLE OF CONTENTS:

1. Excuses: 1
2. Write It Down: 10
3. Confess it: 19
4. Happy: 32
5. Healthy: 39
6. Wealthy: 65
7. Take Action: 80

If you want to lose weight, increase strength, boost energy, build lean muscle, cure illness, sickness, disease, and get my best tips on exercise, nutrition, and supplementation for **free**, simply submit your name and email address right here:

www.FitChristopherMitchell.com

Chapter One:

Excuses!

Did you know that 98% of the world's population is either dead or dead broke at the age of sixty-five? It's sad, but very true. That's crazy when you think about it. How could such a huge percentage of the people in the world be either dead or dead broke at only sixty-five years old? That is so young! Why is it that so many people die so young or never have any money in life? **EXCUSES**, plain and simple!

The only reason in the world why people could possibly be dead or broke at the young age of sixty-five is because of **EXCUSES**. I mean, how could a person not have figured out how to make a lot of money by the age of sixty-five or how could a person not have chosen to take better care of their health so that they would live longer than sixty-five years? The only thing I can possibly think of is that these people made too many **EXCUSES** for too long.

You now know that 98% of the population is dead broke, but did you know that 98% of the population are employees? It's sad, but very true. Now, let me ask you another question. Did you know that only 2% of the population is wealthy? How ironic is it that 2% of the population are business owners? You don't need to be a Harvard graduate to do simple math. If you look at the numbers that I just mentioned you can realize that in order for you to become wealthy you absolutely must be a business owner. This is 100% non-negotiable! Why is it that only 2% of the population own their own business? **EXCUSES**, plain and simple!

Did you know that 75% of the adult population is overweight? This includes people who are twenty years old and upward. This makes me sick! This tells me that people have no respect for themselves. This tells me that people are committing suicide at alarming levels by what they put inside their bodies. What is causing so many people to be fat and out of shape? **EXCUSES**, plain and simple!

Did you know that 32% of people between the ages of eighteen and thirty-four still live at home with their parents? This is pathetic! What the heck are these people doing with their lives to get these kinds of results? What is causing such a huge percentage of grown adults to still be living at home with mommy and daddy? **EXCUSES**, plain and simple!

Did you know that 50% of all marriages end in divorce? Did you know that 67% of second marriages end in divorce? Did you know that 74% of third marriages end in divorce? This is absolute insanity! This is a shame from the pit of hell! Marriage was supposed to last forever, until someone dies, not until you have a bad day, or have an argument, or have a problem in your finances. Why do so many people give up on their soulmate in life? **EXCUSES**, plain and simple!

Did you know that 80% of teenagers in the United States drink alcohol and 43% of them use drugs? How in the world have so many young people succumbed to self-destruction? This fact tells me that their parents are non-existent in their lives. Drugs and alcohol destroy people. This is a guaranteed fact! Why are so many teenagers insecure and giving in to peer pressure at such a young age? **EXCUSES**, plain and simple!

Now, I'm going to share some mind-boggling statistics with you on the number one reason why the majority of people in America will never be happy, healthy, or wealthy. Pay close attention to the information I'm going to share with you right now because it could truly change your life just like it did for me ten years ago. All of the following statistics are from BLS American Time Use Survey, A.C. Nielsen Company.

Did you know that 99% of households in America have at least one TV?

Did you know that the average household has 2.24 TV's?

I want to go on record and state that my home does not have one single TV in it. I haven't had a TV for over ten years and my home will never have a TV in it for the rest of my life.

Did you know that a whopping 65% of houses in America have at least three TV's?

Did you know that 67% of Americans watch TV while eating their dinner?

Did you know that 56% of Americans pay for cable TV?

Did you know that 49% of Americans admit that they watch too much TV? Half of our country says that they watch too much TV, but yet they do absolutely nothing about it.

Did you know that the average American watches 5.11 hours of TV every single day?

-Asian 3.14 hours.
-Hispanic 4.35 hours.
-White 5.02 hours.
-Black 7.12 hours.

Did you know that the average American will waste nine full years of their life watching TV?

Did you know that 54% of four to six year old children in America said that they would rather watch TV than spend time with their fathers?

Did you know that the average American youth is in school 900 hours per year?

Did you know that the average American youth watches 1,200 hours of TV per year?

Did you know that the average American will witness 150,000 violent acts on TV by the time they're only eighteen years old?

Why would anyone ever waste so much of their life watching TV, which does nothing but make them stupid? **EXCUSES**, plain and simple!

I hope you now realize why so many people in America are not happy, healthy, and wealthy? The reason why is **EXCUSES**, plain and simple!

People make excuses as to why they're broke financially. People make excuses as to why they're an employee, rather than an employer. People make excuses as to why they're fat and out of shape. People make excuses as to why they still live at home with their parents. People make excuses as to why they divorced their spouse. People make excuses as to why they drink alcohol and use drugs. People also make excuses as to why they waste so much time watching TV.

However, if you want to become happy, healthy, and wealthy, you absolutely must stop making excuses! An excuse is nothing more than a well planned lie. It's a pathetic, made up reason for you to take your life for granted and waste all of your time.

I'm going to teach you how to become happy, healthy, and wealthy, but you're going to have to put your excuses behind you. You're going to have to stop watching that stupid TV. You're going to have to stop wasting your time. You're going to have to stop procrastinating. You're going to have to start taking action right now! If you're ready to change your life forever, let's begin!

Chapter Two:

Write It Down!

What is your dream? What do you absolutely love to do? What do you focus on and think about most of the time? If you had millions of dollars in your bank account right now what would you do with your time? You have to be able to answer these questions before you can become happy, healthy, and wealthy. If you can't answer these questions off the top of your head right now then I encourage you to stop reading.

Go get a pen and piece of paper and write down EVERYTHING your mind can possibly imagine that you would like to achieve in your life. Focus and visualize in your mind about every single thing you would do if you had all the time and money in the world.

Let your imagination go crazy! Don't worry about how or when it will happen. This time right now is to simply live out all of your wildest goals and dreams in your mind. You have to be able to see yourself doing the things you want to do in your mind before you will ever achieve them in the physical world.

This book is all about how to become happy, healthy, and wealthy. So, start writing down absolutely everything you can think of that would make you happy, healthy, and wealthy.

What would make you happy? Would it be having millions of dollars in the bank? Would it be traveling around the entire world? Would it be writing a best-selling book? Would it be having your skills and wisdom change people's lives? Whatever it is, write it down right now!

What would make you healthy? Would it be to quit smoking? Would it be to quit drinking? Would it be to start eating healthier foods? Would it be to start exercising for thirty minutes every single day? Whatever it is, write it down right now!

What would make you wealthy? Would it be to stop wasting money on worthless things? Would it be to start your own business? Would it be to start investing in real estate? Whatever it is, write it down right now!

Only three out of every one hundred adults write down their goals. Only eight out of every one hundred people write down their resolutions that they set for the new year. Just by writing down your goals makes you 50% more likely to achieve them.

Writing down your goals is the first step in actually achieving them. Since most people never write down their goals, simply by doing so puts you far ahead of the competition. All of the world's most successful people agree that by writing down their goals is a big reason why they achieved the success that they did. Writing down specific goals with a date you want to achieve them by works the best. I always tell people that nothing becomes dynamic until it becomes specific. Write that quote down!

Most people in the world don't even have goals, let alone write them down. A Harvard study discovered that 83% of Americans don't even have any goals. A written goal needs to be carried with you everywhere you go. Look at it throughout the day and meditate on it. Visualize how you will feel once your goal is achieved.

I have a lot of affirmations that I live by. I write them down on notecards and read them every single day. One of my favorite affirmations that I've lived by for a long time is:

A dream without a goal is just a wish!

The goal is the part of the dream that you write down. If you don't write it down then it's nothing more than a wish. Don't leave your dreams in the hands of a wish. Take control of your dreams by writing them down. Remember, that just by writing your goals down you've already increased your chances of achieving them by a whopping 50% compared to those who didn't write them down. That's powerful when you think about it.

People who write down their goals are more successful than those who do not. However, let's look at the results of an actual study:

Dr. Gail Matthews, a psychology professor at the Dominican University in California, recently studied the art and science of goal setting. She put two hundred and sixty-seven people together. This included men and women from all over the world, and from all different walks of life. These people consisted of entrepreneurs, artists, bankers, lawyers, educators, and healthcare professionals.

She divided the participants into two separate groups. One group wrote down their goals and the other group did not write down their goals. She discovered that the group who wrote down their goals achieved them at a much higher level than those who did not write down their goals. In fact, she found that the people who wrote down their goals had a 42% better chance of achieving them than those who did not write them down.

The chances of you achieving your goals increases even more when you share your goals with someone who supports you. Why does writing down your goals have such a profound impact on achieving success?

It has to do with the way our brains work. Your brain has a left and a right hemisphere. The wide, flat bundle of neural fibers that connects the two hemispheres is called the corpus callosum. This is the conduit through which the electrical signals between the right brain, which is imaginative, and the left brain, which is literal, make contact with each other.

These electrical signals then move into the fluid that surrounds the brain and travels up and down the spinal column. These signals then start communicating with every cell, fiber, and bone in our bodies to the consciousness that operates within us to transform our thoughts into reality. It allows us to properly align our frequency to the lifestyle that we truly dream of.

This is powerful because if you only think about your goals instead of writing them down you're only using the right hemisphere of your brain, which is your imaginative center. However, if you think about your goals AND write them down you're then tapping into the power of the left hemisphere of your brain. This sends a signal to your consciousness and every cell in your body that you're going to achieve your goals and dreams no matter what.

Just by writing down your goals will send a totally new dimension of ideas and productivity to your powerful subconscious mind.

Writing down your goals is a simple way of taking action, but can have a huge impact on the amount of success that you achieve in your life. Studies have proven that people who write down their goals in life are way more successful than people who do not write down their goals. Everyone in the world knows this, but very few actually do it. Be the exception to this rule and you'll definitely stand out in the crowds that surround you.

Start writing down all of your goals and dreams that you have on how you can become happier, healthier, and wealthier right now. Don't wait another minute. Don't procrastinate any longer. Do it right now!

Chapter Three:

Confess it!

The Law Of Confession states that the words you speak will manifest in your life because words are seeds.

Believing and then speaking the word of God is a very powerful law that can truly change your life. God created the entire universe simply by speaking words. See for yourself:

God said, let there be light and there was light. **Genesis 1:3**

God said, let there be a vault between the waters to separate water from water. **Genesis 1:6**

God said, let the water under the sky be gathered to one place and let dry ground appear. **Genesis 1:9**

God said, let the land produce vegetation; seed bearing plants and trees on the land that bear fruit with seed in it according to their various kinds. **Genesis 1:11**

God said, let there be lights in the vault of the sky to separate the day from the night, and let them serve as signs to mark sacred times, days and years, and let them be lights in the vault of the sky to give light on the earth. **Genesis 1:14-15**

God said, let the water teem with living creatures and let birds fly above the earth across the vault of the sky. **Genesis 1:20**

God said, let the land produce living creatures according to their kinds: the livestock, the creatures that move along the ground, and the wild animals each according to its kind. **Genesis 1:24**

God said, let us make mankind in our image, in our likeness, so that they may rule over the fish in the sea and the birds in the sky, over the livestock and all the wild animals, and over all the creatures that move along the ground. **Genesis 1:26**

This is amazing! Not only did God create the entire universe simply by speaking it into existence, but he created us in his image and likeness. That means he gave us the same exact power and authority with the words that we speak. Our words have amazing power. Our words can literally change any circumstance in our lives. That's why it's extremely important to only speak about things that you want. Never speak about things that you don't want. The words that you speak will manifest in your life. You have to confess only what you want in life.

Growing up as children we always heard the saying: sticks and stones will break my bones, but words will never hurt me.

As adults, we know the complete opposite is true. Sticks and stones have never broken any bones, but hurtful words have been known to cause all kinds of illness, sickness, disease, poverty, and unhappiness. Some people have even committed suicide because of the power of hurtful words spoken to them.

Children who have parents that speak negatively to them all the time grow up with inferiority complexes. If you're a parent make sure that you only speak positive words to your children. Encourage them with your words. Remind them with your words that they're blessed and that they can achieve anything they set their mind to. Build them up with your words rather than tearing them down. The words that you speak to your children will either propel them forward or make them go backward.

Do you ever notice that poor people always say things like:

-I can't afford that.

-Money is the root of all evil.

-Money doesn't grow on trees.

-I'd rather be happy than be rich.

Every time a person confesses something negative about money they're only cursing themselves financially. They're making a guarantee to themselves that they will be broke forever. If you say that you can't afford something you're absolutely right. The words that you confess will manifest in your life.

Instead of confessing how broke you are all the time, start confessing how rich you are. Jesus came to give us life and give it to us in abundance. Abundance isn't living broke! Abundance is living rich. Abundance is having more than enough. Abundance is having so much that your cup runs over. You deserve to live a life of absolute abundance.

Start confessing what The Bible says about your happiness instead of what the world says. Start confessing what The Bible says about your health instead of what the world says. Start confessing what The Bible says about your wealth instead of what the world says. Start confessing God's word over your life and no matter what is going on around you it will have no choice but to change and do what you're confessing.

You don't need to know how your life will change. All you need to know is that by confessing God's word it will change any situation in the natural world if you'll simply believe what you confess. That's how the Law Of Confession works. Your words have power, but unfortunately most people only confess what they see, not what they want. Let's see what The Bible says about the power of the words that we confess:

My word that goes out from my mouth will not return to me empty, but will accomplish what I desire and achieve the purpose for which I sent it. **Isaiah 55:11**

The tongue has the power of life and death, and those who love it will eat it's fruit. **Proverbs 18:21**

By your words you will be acquitted, and by your words you will be condemned. **Matthew 12:37**

If I say to this mountain, go throw yourself into the sea, and do not doubt in my heart, but believe what I say will happen, it will be done for me. **Mark 11:23**

I give life to the dead and call into being things that were not.
Romans 4:17

Do not let any unwholesome talk come out of your mouth, but only what is helpful for building others up according to their needs, that it may benefit those who listen.
Ephesians 4:29

I remember confessing when I was only seventeen years old that I was going to become a professional fitness model and appear on the covers of fitness magazines all over the world. Every single person that knew me laughed at me and told me I was crazy. However, I kept confessing over and over to myself every single day that I would appear on the covers of fitness magazines. A year and a half later at the age of eighteen I appeared on my first magazine cover. I had spoken that into existence just like God spoke the entire universe into existence.

If you have a car loan, a mortgage loan, or credit card loans, that means you're in debt! Use The Law Of Confession to get yourself out of debt. Take your car loan, your mortgage loan, and your credit card loans and confess over them. Listen up car loan, I command that you be completely paid off in the name of Jesus! Listen up mortgage loan, I command that you be completely paid off in the name of Jesus! Listen up credit card loans, I command that you be completely paid off in the name of Jesus!

Use The Law Of Confession to bring in more money. Open up your empty purse or wallet and confess over it. Listen up purse, I decree and declare that you are now filled with hundred dollar bills. I command that you over flow with money. I confess that I receive money from the north, south, east, and west.

Use The Law Of Confession to reprogram your poverty mindset into a prosperous mindset. Look yourself in the mirror every single day and repeat out loud: I am rich! I am wealthy! I am successful! I am prosperous! Money comes to me easily and abundantly every single day! My sales are increasing every single day! New opportunities come to me every single day! I am rich in every way so that I can be generous on every occasion. I am an expert in my field! I am a Multi-Millionaire!

Don't think you're too good to look at yourself in the mirror and talk to yourself like this. Look at the power of what your words can do. The words you confess can absolutely make you happy. The words you confess can absolutely make you healthy. The words you confess can absolutely make you wealthy. In The Bible Jesus knew how powerful his words were. He killed a fig tree by speaking to it. Look at this:

The next day as they were leaving Bethany, Jesus was hungry. Seeing in the distance a fig tree in leaf, he went to find out if it had any fruit. When he reached it he found nothing but leaves because it was not the season for figs. Then he said to the tree, may no one ever eat fruit from you again. And his disciples heard him say it. **Mark 11:12-14**

Believe it, then speak it! Your words can change your entire life. The power of your words is beyond comprehending. Confessing the word of God over your life will change any circumstance you might be dealing with. There is nothing in the entire world that cannot be turned around by the power of your words. Most Christians don't understand the connection between the words they speak and the life they live. Jesus said it like this:

The Spirit gives life, the flesh counts for nothing. The words I have spoken to you, they are full of the Spirit and life. **John 6:63**

If any area of your life needs turned around start confessing the word of God over it. Tap into this ancient Biblical secret and watch your life transform in every area.

Law: If you want to become happy, healthy, and wealthy, you must only confess what you want in life! Never confess what you don't want!

Chapter Four:

Happy!

In this chapter, I'm going to share my own personal opinion with you of my thirty-eight years of living in nine different states and meeting thousands and thousands of people. If you walk out of the house in the morning and come across people it is quite evident that most people are not happy. Most people hate their job. They hate their commute to their job. They hate the amount of money they make at their job. They hate how much time their job takes away from the things they would rather be doing in life. They hate the house they live in. They hate the car they drive. In a nutshell, they just down right hate their lives. I truly believe that 98% of all the people in the world are not happy.

In my opinion, I believe that most people are unhappy in life because they spend most of their time at a job every day that they hate. They're not spending their time on what they're truly passionate about. They gave up on their dreams in life and settled for a nine to five job just so they can get a paycheck to pay their bills. That would make me unhappy too, which is why I'll never work at a job for someone else. Working at a job is the same exact thing as slavery. Who the heck would be happy as a slave?

However, if you're currently at a job that you hate then it's up to you to change it. No one else can change your life and make you happy except you. You have to take responsibility for why you're unhappy. You have to take responsibility for that job you hate because you're the one who chose to work there. It was your choice! If you hate your job and it makes you unhappy then it's up to you to leave and start doing what truly makes you happy.

That's all there is to it! If you choose to stay at that job that makes you unhappy then you give up your right to complain about it. Stop doing what makes you unhappy or shut up! The majority of the people in the world work at a dead end job every day that they hate, but then they do nothing to change it. All they do is complain about it to anyone who will listen.

Studies show, and I think that most people agree that the top three things that make people happy are:

1. Good relationships.

2. Work you're passionate about.

3. Giving of yourself to others.

I definitely agree that I'm happy when I'm around people that I love and care about. My wife and my daughter are the two most important people in the world to me, besides God of course. When I'm spending time with them I'm happy. It doesn't matter what we're doing together, I'm just happy being with them. I also have close friends from my church that I'm happy being around as well.

As for number two, yes, I definitely agree again. I see how unhappy so many people are with their daily work that it's easy to recognize the few people who are happy with what they do. I am most certainly happy being an Author and Speaker. I love it so much that I would, and have done it for free. The truth about you being happy in your work is if you would do it for free. I have a few people now and then tell me that they love their job. I then turn around and tell them no they don't. After going back and forth for a minute I silence them with this question; If your job didn't pay you would you work there for free?

What do you think the answer is 100% of the time? Absolutely not! I then say, see I told you so. If you wouldn't do your job for free then you don't love what you do. If you ask any successful person if they would do what they currently do for free every single one of them would tell you yes. That's how they became successful, by doing what they love. Successful people do what they love and the money always chases after them. Broke people do the opposite. They chase after money and the money always out runs them. If you do what you love and are passionate about it you'll never have to work a day of your life.

I have to definitely agree with number three as well. Everything I've done in my entire life I've always done so I could be a blessing to others. I write my books to share what I know with the world. I love helping people lose weight. I love helping people write their own books. I love inspiring people to change their lives.

I love making money because I love giving money to others. The more money I bring in the more money I can give out. I get thank you emails and testimonials from people all over the world after they read one of my books. This tells me that what I do is definitely my calling in life because of the joy it brings me when I hear how much my work benefits others.

So, if you want to be happy in life you need to develop good relationships with people who have the same interests that you do. If you hate what you do for a living then you absolutely must quit and start doing what you love. Otherwise, you will never be happy. And of course, if you want to be happy you need to think about others and give of your time, money, and effort. Start doing these three things and you will never be unhappy again.

Chapter Five:

Healthy!

In case you didn't know, I was a Professional Nutritionist and Certified Personal Trainer for over twenty years. During that time, I helped thousands of people lose weight, gain muscle, increase their energy, and eliminate their prescription drugs that were killing them. When it comes to living a healthy lifestyle, I'm an absolute expert. I also competed in several bodybuilding competitions and was a professional fitness model for many years as well.

I don't share that to brag or try to impress you, but simply to impress upon you that what I'm about to teach you in this chapter will turn you into a perfectly healthy human being. The information I'm going to share with you right now will help you lose weight faster than anything else in the world, will boost your energy, help you increase lean muscle, and will add many years to your lifespan, if you implement it of course. If you're ready to learn what the right foods to eat are, which natural supplements work for long term health, how often you should exercise, along with an actual workout regimen to follow, then let's begin the journey to perfect health.

The first thing I want to teach you about living a healthy lifestyle is a different pattern of eating. Americans are fat because they don't know how to eat properly. They eat non-stop. Not only do they never stop eating, but they never eat the right foods. By the time you finish this chapter, you'll be an expert when it comes to proper nutrition.

To lose weight fast, you want to start incorporating something called Intermittent Fasting into your daily lifestyle. In case you've never heard about Intermittent Fasting before, let me give you some history about it so you can see the amazing benefits it can provide for you and your health.

Intermittent Fasting is an eating pattern where you cycle between periods of eating and fasting. There are two different intermittent fasting methods, both of which split the day or week into eating periods and fasting periods.

Most people think of religion when they think of the word fasting. I know I first did. Throughout my childhood, I had a friend in my neighborhood who would sometimes not eat when everyone else did. I asked him why he wasn't eating and he always responded with, I'm fasting. Now granted, he was fasting as part of his religion, but today people are starting to fast more than ever before because of a lot of different health benefits. Here are just a few of the amazing health benefits you can receive from Intermittent Fasting:

-helps prevent cancer.

-reduces inflammation.

-benefits brain function.

-decreases insulin levels.

-boosts your metabolism.

-helps prevent Alzheimer's disease.

-removes waste material from cells.

-lowers your risk of getting diabetes.

-Insulin levels decrease significantly.

-lowers your risk of getting heart disease.

-Growth Hormone levels increase significantly.

-changes the function of cells, genes, and hormones.

-speeds up the fat burning and muscle building process.

-makes your stored body fat more accessible for energy.

-strengthens your immune system and helps you live a longer lifespan.

Did you read that? Intermittent Fasting will help you live LONGER!

If you've ever read the Holy Bible before, you know that some people lived for nine hundred years. How was that possible and why is the average person only living about seventy-five years today? Well, the people in the Holy Bible were actually doing Intermittent Fasting thousands of years ago. They would go days and weeks without eating. You'll notice that the people in the Holy Bible:

-Never Got Sick.

-Never Lacked Energy.

-Never Went To A Doctor.

-Never Ate Fast Food Or Sugar.

-Fasted For Days And Weeks At A Time.

-Walked (Exercised) Everywhere They Went.

-Had Lifespans That Lasted Hundreds And Hundreds Of Years.

So, Intermittent Fasting has been around since BC. However, our culture that we live in today has brainwashed us from the day we were born and most people are very close minded to trying something different, like Intermittent Fasting.

The results from thousands of years prove Intermittent Fasting works great for losing weight and building lean muscle fast. I'm proof of that! Intermittent Fasting has not only changed my physical body on the outside, but it has truly changed my internal health as well. There's two main ways to do Intermittent Fasting:

-Choose two days per week and eat nothing on those two days. This is a twenty-four hour fast, twice a week. This option requires two days per week without eating anything.

-Don't eat anything for sixteen hours of the day, every single day of the week. Eat all of your meals in an eight-hour time period each day.

This second option is the option I live by. I eat all my meals every single day between 2pm-10pm. The remaining sixteen hours I don't eat anything.

Intermittent Fasting has a lot of health benefits, but the greatest two benefits it provides is the huge effect that it has on the production of two hormones in your body: Insulin and Growth Hormone.

Intermittent Fasting decreases your Insulin levels, which is good because that means you're lowering your bodyfat percentage.

Intermittent Fasting increases your Growth Hormone levels, which is good because that means you're increasing your energy, your strength, and your muscle mass.

I personally believe the huge increase in my Growth Hormone levels provided by Intermittent Fasting is what has allowed me to stay lean and muscular all year long. Intermittent Fasting helps a person lose weight and increase muscle mass faster than anything else I've ever witnessed. Out of all the weight loss secrets that I've ever learned, I would have to say that Intermittent Fasting is number one.

Now that you know what Intermittent Fasting is, let me give you my personal nutritional regimen so you can see how to incorporate it into your own daily lifestyle. This daily nutritional regimen will help you lose weight, build lean muscle, increase energy, and cure illness, sickness, and disease. I'm currently thirty-eight years old. I never get sick or lack energy, and I haven't been to a Doctor in over twenty years. My personal nutritional regimen keeps me perfectly healthy and it will do the same for you. Flip over to the next page and you'll see my exact nutritional regimen that I follow daily.

As soon as I wake up in the morning:

I mix one scoop of *Green Juice* in eight ounces of water.

I then drink my fat melting Hot Chocolate, which contains:

2 tbs of Cacao Powder.

4 tbs of Raw Honey.

1 tsp of Ground Cinnamon.

1 tsp of Ground Turmeric.

1 tsp of Ground Nutmeg.

Thirty minutes after I wake up in the morning, I go to the gym and do my cardio and resistance training on an empty stomach. I cover myself in sweats so I can keep my body temperature high.

I eat an Intermittent Fasting lifestyle for all my meals. I consume all my food between 2pm-10pm.

Meal 1 at 2:00 pm:

Mix the following in a bowl with hot water.

2 tbs of Flaxseed.

2 tbs of Chia Seeds.

2 servings of Fresh Fruit.

1 cup of Oatmeal.

Meal 2 at 5:00 pm:

Mix the following in a Vitamix:

Spinach, Cucumber, Orange, Apple, Pineapple, Strawberries, Blueberries.

1 scoop of *Green Juice*.

2 scoops of *Complete Protein*.

24oz of cold water.

You can get the products *Green Juice* and *Complete Protein* here: www.LoseWeightProtein.com

Meal 3 at 8:00 pm:

Mix the following in a bowl:

Spinach, Tomato, Black Beans, Veggie Burgers, Tortilla Chips, and Apple Cider Vinegar for a dressing.

Before I go to sleep at night:

I drink my fat melting Hot Chocolate, which contains:

2 tbs of Cacao Powder.

4 tbs of Raw Honey.

1 tsp of Ground Cinnamon.

1 tsp of Ground Turmeric.

1 tsp of Ground Nutmeg.

I also drink one gallon of water filled with Lemons every day. This gives me energy, helps me lose bodyfat, and strengthens my immune system.

Now that you know the right foods to eat with the right eating pattern, let me talk to you about how to get the most out of your cardio. HIIT- High Intensity Interval Training! To lose weight fast, you want to do HIIT for your cardio. HIIT is a way of doing cardio with short bursts of high intensity energy (exercising) followed by short bursts of low intensity energy (resting).

HIIT is designed to get your heart rate elevated very quickly for a minute or two, then bring your heart rate back down to normal by resting for a minute or two. If you did a cardio session for twenty minutes with one minute intervals then your actual cardio (exercise) time would only be ten minutes long.

Can you imagine doing only ten minutes of cardio a few days a week and losing weight effortlessly? Believe me, it's possible! Let me give you an example of a HIIT session:

Let's say you're using the treadmill for a twenty-minute cardio session. Let's say you run really quickly (exercise) for one minute, followed by walking very slowly (resting) for one minute. You would do this interval sequence of one minute fast followed by one minute slow the entre twenty minutes.

Cardio goes by very quickly when you do HIIT. Not only that, but what makes HIIT so powerful for losing weight is the after-burn effect. The after-burn effect is all the calories you burn after your cardio session is over.

You see, by getting your heart rate up for one minute, then bringing it back down for one minute, followed by taking it back up for one minute, then bringing it back down for one minute, you're actually confusing your heart rate. It doesn't know whether to go up or go down. So, after your twenty-minute cardio session is over the weight loss process is far from being over. The weight loss process has only just begun because since you confused your heart rate your body is going to continue to burn fat for the next twenty-four hours straight, even while you're sleeping!

You'll start noticing every morning when you get out of bed that you're leaner than you were the night before. This is because your body was burning calories all night long while you were sleeping. That's the amazing benefit of doing HIIT type cardio sessions. With HIIT you get to burn a lot more calories by doing a lot less cardio. For fast weight loss, simply do a twenty to thirty minute HIIT session a few times per week.

Resistance Training With Weights is next. To lose weight, build lean muscle, increase your energy, and increase your strength, you want to start incorporating resistance training into your lifestyle. In case you've never trained with weights before, let me give you a little history.

Resistance training is the use of resistance to muscular contraction to help a person burn fat, lose weight, increase strength, boost energy, and build lean muscle mass. There are four different forms of resistance training: free weights, resistance bands, weighted machines, and your own bodyweight.

Resistance training will not only help you lose weight, build lean muscle, increase your energy, and increase your strength, but it has a lot of health healing benefits as well:

-reduces insomnia.

-improves posture.

-strengthens joints.

-improves flexibility.

-boosts energy levels.

-improves your mood.

-protects bone health.

-increases confidence.

-increases sperm count.

-decreases arthritis pain.

-alleviates low back pain.

-sharpens concentration.

-reduces type 2 diabetes.

-fights against depression.

- improves blood circulation.

- lowers high blood pressure.

- prevents erectile dysfunction.

- decreases risk of osteoporosis.

- strengthens the immune system.

- improves balance & coordination.

On top of all of these health healing benefits, resistance training also has some powerful weight loss properties as well:

- increases fat oxidation by increasing your body's heat production.

- increases your metabolism by replacing bodyfat with lean muscle.
- releases fat burning hormones because of the increase in your natural testosterone & growth hormone levels.

-increases your energy, which will turn up thermogenesis in your body.

So far in this chapter I've taught you about Intermittent Fasting, I've given you my actual nutritional regimen, I've educated you on the best type of cardio to do, which is high intensity interval training, and now I'm going to lay out three different exercise regimens. You can follow the one that's best suited for you.

If you consider yourself to be at the Beginner level (you have a lot of weight to lose and you don't know much about working out) then I encourage you to follow this walking exercise routine I've put together for you. This will allow you to get some exercise, but nothing too strenuous that you can't follow through with.

Beginner level exercise routine:

Monday: 20 minutes of interval based walking. I want you to walk very quickly for 1 minute, then I want you to walk very slowly for 1 minute. I want you to do this for 20 minutes. Congratulate yourself when you're done! You are now one day closer to becoming perfectly healthy.

Wednesday: 20 minutes of interval based walking. I want you to walk very quickly for 1 minute, then I want you to walk very slowly for 1 minute. I want you to do this for 20 minutes. Congratulate yourself when you're done! You are now one day closer to becoming perfectly healthy.

Friday: 20 minutes of interval based walking. I want you to walk very quickly for 1 minute, then I want you to walk very slowly for 1 minute. I want you to do this for 20 minutes.

Congratulate yourself when you're done! You are now one day closer to becoming perfectly healthy.

You can substitute another form of cardio for walking if you want to. Switch it up sometimes and do the treadmill one day, the stationary bike one day, and the elliptical one day. That's three different workouts per week. Every single twenty minute cardio session you complete is getting you closer to becoming perfectly healthy.

Just take it one day at a time. As you begin to lose weight and gain mobility you can then move up to the Intermediate level routine. Congratulations! I'm proud of you!

If you consider yourself to be at the Intermediate level (you've worked out before, you might even belong to a gym, but you're not very comfortable lifting weights by yourself) then I encourage you to follow this machine based exercise routine I've put together for you.

Intermediate level exercise routine:

ALL exercises are on machines.

Monday: Chest, Shoulders & Triceps.

Seated Chest Press: 3 sets by 20, 15, 12 (add weight each set).

Seated Shoulder Press: 3 sets by 20, 15, 12 (add weight each set).

Seated Tricep Press: 3 sets by 20, 15, 12 (add weight each set).

Wednesday: Quadriceps, Hamstrings, Glutes & Calves.

Seated Leg Press: 3 sets by 20, 15, 12 (add weight each set).

Seated Leg Curl: 3 sets by 20, 15, 12 (add weight each set).

Seated Leg Extension: 3 sets by 20, 15, 12 (add weight each set).

Leg Press Calf Raises: 3 sets by 20, 15, 12 (add weight each set).

Friday: Back, Biceps & Forearms.

Lat Pulldown: 3 sets by 20, 15, 12 (add weight each set).

Seated Row: 3 sets by 20, 15, 12 (add weight each set).

Seated Curls: 3 sets by 20, 15, 12 (add weight each set).

Each day that you work out is getting you closer to becoming perfectly healthy. Just take it one day at a time. Congratulations! I'm proud of you!

If you consider yourself to be at the Advanced level (this means you exercise regularly, you're comfortable working out with free weights by yourself, and you only have 10-20 pounds to lose), then I encourage you to follow this free weight exercise routine I've put together for you.

Advanced level exercise routine:

Deadlifts- The Entire Body

Dips- Chest, Shoulders & Triceps

Pull Ups- Back, Biceps & Forearms

Barefoot Barbell Calf Raises- Calves

Lying Leg Curls- Hamstrings & Calves

Push Ups- Chest, Shoulders & Triceps

Leg Presses- Quadriceps, Hamstrings & Glutes

Bicep Curls (DB or Barbell)- Biceps & Forearms

Shoulder Presses (DB or Barbell)- Shoulders & Triceps

Deep Barbell Squats- Quadriceps, Hamstrings & Glutes

Bench Presses (DB or Barbell)- Chest, Shoulders & Triceps

The above exercises that I just shared with you are the cream of the crop for losing weight and sculpting lean muscle mass.

Monday: Chest, Shoulders & Triceps.

Push Ups: 3 sets to failure (bodyweight only).

Barbell Bench Presses: 4 sets by 20, 15, 12, 8 (add weight each set).

Seated Barbell Presses: 3 sets by 15, 12, 8 (add weight each set).

Wednesday: Quadriceps, Hamstrings, Glutes & Calves.

Leg Presses: 4 sets by 20, 15, 12, 8 (add weight each set).

Lying Leg Curls: 3 sets by 20, 15, 12 (add weight each set).

Barefoot Barbell Calf Raises: 2 sets by 20, 15 (add weight each set).

Friday: Back, Biceps & Forearms.

Deadlifts: 3 sets by 15, 12, 8 (add weight each set).

Lat Pulldown: 3 sets by 20, 15, 12 (add weight each set).

Seated DB Curls: 3 sets by 15, 12, 8 (add weight each set).

Every workout that you complete is getting you closer to becoming perfectly healthy. There will be days when you don't feel like working out, but stay committed to reaching your goals, and the results you achieve will be well worth it. Congratulations! I'm proud of you!

Chapter Six:

Wealthy!

Everyone wants to be wealthy, but only 2% ever will. This simply comes down to facts. Numbers never lie. Like I said in chapter one the only way to become wealthy is to own your own business. You must be the boss. You must be the one in control. In order to become wealthy, you must be in control of your time and money. This is 100% non-negotiable!

Let me explain to you how a job actually operates. Your job was created by the owner. The owner is an entrepreneur. An entrepreneur is someone who starts their own business because they want to become wealthy. In order for them to make more money they have to increase the size of their business.

When their business grows they have to hire employees to help keep up with the increased workload. The business owner loves the increased workload because that means more money. However, what the business owner does not love is YOU, the employee. An employee to a business owner is nothing more than a headache. If a business owner has one employee then that means he has one headache. If a business owner has one hundred employees then that means he is running an adult daycare center.

The only reason a business owner will hire employees is because they can't do all the work by themselves. So, they hire employees to delegate the workload. However, since the business owner now has to take some of his money to pay the employees with, this means it will take him longer to accumulate wealth. The business owner will pay the employees the very least amount that he can so that he can keep as much of the money for himself as he can. The business owner will pay the employees only as much as he has to just to keep the employees coming back to work every day. This is how Corporate America works. If you don't like it, then change it.

That's why it is impossible to become wealthy working as an employee for someone else. An employee is not in control of how much money they earn. Their boss is. A business owner will never pay an employee millions of dollars. That's the reason why they started their business to begin with. They started their own business because they wanted to become wealthy. They want to keep the money for themselves.

So, hopefully now you understand why it's absolutely impossible to become wealthy as an employee. If you don't own the business then that means you don't call the shots. If you don't call the shots then you have no control over how much money you can earn. The business owner tells you how much he'll pay you and you either take it or go find another job. Employees have no negotiating power. He who makes all the money makes all the rules. Deal with it!

If you want to become wealthy you absolutely must start your own business. There is no other way around it. Unless of course you want to hope and pray you win the lottery. I can't imagine why a person would rather work at a dead end job with no chance of becoming wealthy than to start their own business and just work hard until it pays off.

If you're like most employees, you might be saying to yourself right now, well Christopher, I would love to start my own business, but I don't have any money for that. If you just said that to yourself then you've assumed that it costs a lot of money to start a business. I'm here to tell you that it doesn't. I've started at least twenty businesses throughout my life. Most of these businesses cost me less than $500 to get started.

However, my latest and greatest business was a gift from almighty God in Heaven above. That's what I'm going to share with you in this chapter. I absolutely love helping people. I love sharing what I know with others. That's why I write books. My books can reach people all over the world, which they have. I hope this book changes your life. I know it can, but you've got to be the one who does the work. I've already taught you how to become happy and healthy, and now in this chapter I'm going to teach you how to become wealthy.

Would you believe me if I told you I know of a business that you can start right now, right in the comfort of your own home for only $20? Well, do you believe me? If you found out that I'm telling you the truth would you get started immediately? I promise you what I'm about to teach you is real. It's 100% real. I know because it's the exact business that changed my life. It's the exact business that I'm working on right now as I write this book. Are you ready to find out how you can start your own business and change your life with only $20? Here's the answer: **WRITE A BOOK!** Writing a book can be a very lucrative business.

My books are a big source of the money I earn. I've written and self-published more than twenty books. Since that's what I've become good at, I can now share my expertise with you. I can teach you how to do the same thing that I've done. You can only be at one place at a time, but your books can be all over the world at the same time.

Don't worry, it's nothing like what you think it is. Writing and publishing a book is ten times easier and ten times less expensive than you think it is. This is exactly what I did on a part time basis with only $20. It changed my life forever! Starting your own book publishing company is nothing more than writing a book and selling it on Amazon. Let me give you some proven statistics that will hopefully inspire you and motivate you to start writing a book immediately.

-99.75% of the world's population has had a thought at some point in their lives to write a book.

-However, less than 1% of the world's population ever does.

-Out of the less than 1% of people who have written a book, only six out of every one thousand ever publish their book and sell a single copy.

-Out of the few published authors in the world that do write and publish a book, the average book only sells seventy-five copies in a lifetime.

If you make it past the four stages listed above, you are now in a very elite group of people that consists of less than 1/1000th of 1% of the world's population.

Now, hopefully these numbers don't scare you, but instead, inspire you and highly motivate you. Here's why:

It isn't hard to reach this milestone at all. You see, 99.9999% of the world's population give up on their dream of ever writing a book. The reason why they give up is because of some type of ridiculous fear that keeps them from taking action.

There's only three things you need to do in order to write a book and become a published author:

1. Sit down and write your book.

2. Submit and publish your book on Amazon.

3. Learn some marketing tips on how to generate traffic to your book.

The great news is that I can teach you how to do all three very easily. I've written books on **EXACTLY** how to write, edit, publish, and sell your books on Amazon in record time.

If you can read, which you obviously can since you're reading this book right now, then you can write a book. I have two books that are short and straight to the point. They will teach you EXACTLY what you need to know from start to finish. I wrote, edited, published, and even sold my first book ever in less than 48 hours. That was without any help, knowledge, or mentorship whatsoever.

However, you don't have to go through the process alone like I did. I've taken all of my knowledge and expertise and put it inside of two books to help you avoid the same mistakes that I had to overcome. My books will teach you how to write and publish your very first book in record time. I've made the process so simple that **ANYONE** can do it. All you have to do is follow the easy step by step instructions in my two books:

1. Sell Your First Book!

2. How To Make Money As An Author Selling Your Books On Amazon!

You can get both books on Amazon:
www.amazon.com/author/fitchristophermitchell

These books have already helped thousands of people from all walks of life become Published Authors. They're now making money from their books on Amazon. They're so excited! They never thought they could write and publish a book so easily until they read my two books. If they can do it, so can you. The only thing keeping you from becoming a Published Author is taking action. You have absolutely nothing to lose, but possibly a world of opportunity to gain. Let me share with you a few of the many amazing reasons why you should write and publish a book as soon as possible:

1. Writing and publishing your first book will give you instant authority and credibility. When you become a Published Author, people will see you as an expert in your field. People then value your opinion and look to you as a reliable source of information.

2. Writing and publishing your first book will give you the opportunity to change millions of people's lives all over the world. You're only one person, and therefore can only be at one place at one time. However, you can share yourself with the entire world through a published book.

3. Writing and publishing your first book will put you in front of people you never would have had a chance to get in front of before. Rich and successful people read books. If people like your book they will contact you. Some of these people

might pay you a lot of money for a speaking engagement that they're in charge of. As a Published Author, you're now in a highly respected position where you have the ability to create change in the world.

4. Writing and publishing your first book can give you media coverage for your work as an expert in your field. Journalists, Reporters, and Bloggers are always looking for credible people to provide valuable information to their audience. As a Published Author, you can have media coverage circulating around about who you are. It can lead to interviews and being featured in articles.

5. Writing and publishing your first book can attract new clients to you resulting in more money. As a Published Author people will want to do business with you and new

business opportunities can come your way that previously would have been unavailable to you.

6. Writing and publishing your first book can build your business or give you the opportunity to start a business. As a Published Author, your book can now be used as a marketing tool to sell your other products and services. Your book enhances your reputation and gives you more value in the marketplace.

7. Writing and publishing your first book immediately gives you another stream of income. A stream of residual income. That's the best kind of income in the world. Imagine publishing a book just one time, but five years later you're still receiving paychecks for that book. Less than 2% of the world's population earn residual income.

I hope you see the value in becoming a Published Author. Doors will open for you that never would have opened for you otherwise. Having a published book can make you more money, possibly a lot of money. Every single time you write another book you give yourself a raise.

I just taught you how to start your own business for only $20. By the way, the $20 is what it costs for you to have your book cover designed. I share that with you in my books too. Now you know how to become wealthy. It's up to you to take action so you can change your life, or you can do nothing and your life will stay the same. It's time for you to write your first book. Both of my books will help you. They're available to you right now simply by clicking this link:
www.amazon.com/author/fitchristophermitchell

Chapter Seven:

Take Action!

The only way a person can become happy, healthy, and wealthy in life is to take action. No one ever did anything great by sitting back and taking life easy. Only 2% of the world's population is wealthy and for good reason. Only 2% of the world's population take action and make things happen. The other 98% sit around and complain about the wealthy. Instead of complaining about the wealthy, join us! There's plenty of money to go around.

If you want to lose weight, make more money, improve your marriage, or travel the world, you're going to have to start taking action right now! You will never accomplish anything in life by sitting around hoping, wishing, praying, or complaining. You must take action! You have to get off of your lazy butt and make a move.

If you want to lose weight you must follow a healthy nutritional regimen and start exercising. If you want to make more money you must start your own business. If you want to improve your marriage you must spend time with your spouse and possibly get counseling. If you want to travel the world you must come up with a game plan to make it happen.

Everything that I've ever achieved in my life I did by taking massive action. In February of 1996, I wanted to become a professional fitness model. So, I immediately started studying exercise, nutrition, supplementation, and anything else that would bring me closer to achieving this goal. A little over a year and a half later, I appeared on the cover of my first fitness magazine. I would go on to appear in over one hundred fitness magazines around the world.

All my friends and family members laughed at me. They said, no one at my size could ever appear on the cover of a fitness magazine. They said, no one from the tiny town of Marion, Ohio could ever appear on the cover of a fitness magazine. They said, you'll never succeed. You don't have an agent and no one knows who you are. I'm glad I took action instead of listening to them.

My entire life I always wanted to live in Hollywood and work on the sets of major films with the stars. A week after I graduated high school, without telling anyone, I loaded up my car and drove across the country to California by myself. I didn't know a single person in Los Angeles. Once I arrived, I set my mind on getting into Hollywood. I asked around and started taking action. My first break came when I worked on the movie "Gigli", starring Ben Affleck and Jennifer Lopez. This was the movie that I earned my SAG card on. I would go on to meet and work alongside Tom Hanks, Jon Voight, Sigourney Weaver, Ben Affleck, Jennifer Lopez, Suge Knight, Tori Spelling, Melissa Joan Hart, Burt Reynolds, Rob Schneider, Anastacia, Nick Cannon, Sylvester Stallone, and the entire cast of Friends to name a few.

When people from my hometown found out that I moved to Los Angeles they thought I was crazy. A couple years later when they saw me in films and TV shows they wouldn't leave me alone. I'm glad I took action instead of listening to them.

I wanted to write a book many years ago, but never did. I finally took action and now I'm publishing a new book every single week, and my books are selling all over the world. I've had people buy my books in Canada, Germany, Switzerland, India, Australia, and United Kingdom to name a few. My books have also sold in practically every state in America as well. Even though it was always my goal to help people all over the world, I never imagined I would be selling books all over the world. This only happened because I decided to stop making excuses and started taking massive action.

I'm glad you purchased this book. I know you don't know this, but I give 25% of the profits from every book I sell to a non-profit charity to help free under age sex slaves and feed hungry women and their children who have been abandoned. So, thank you very much. I hope you received value from this book, but now that you've read it you have to take it a step further. Don't be like a lot of book buyers who read it, but never take action after they read it.

The number one thing you must do to become successful in life is to take massive action. That's what separates the 2% of the wealthy class from the 98% of the broke class. Whatever your goal is you must take action and you need to do it right now. The longer you procrastinate the longer it will take you to become successful.

In order for you to take action you need to know what area's you need to take action in and then write down a game plan for yourself to follow. Remember, just by writing it down puts you 50% ahead of everyone else.

-Do you need to create a new morning ritual so that you're more productive? If so, write it down and start taking action!

-Do you need to lose some weight so you can become healthier and live longer? If so, write it down and start taking action!

-Do you need to get out of debt so you're not stressed out all the time? If so, write it down and start taking action!

-Do you need to get out of the house and meet some new people? If so, write it down and start taking action!

-Do you need to start being nicer to your spouse and appreciating them more often? If so, write it down and start taking action!

-Do you need to stop taking so many prescriptions that you know are bad for you? If so, write it down and start taking action!

-Do you need to quit your job and start doing what you're truly passionate about? If so, write it down and start taking action!

-Do you need to stop drinking alcohol so you can start enjoying life and the people around you more often? If so, write it down and start taking action!

-Do you need to make more money so you can travel the world? If so, write it down and start taking action!

-Do you need to write your first book so someone else can benefit from it? If so, write it down and start taking action!

Whatever it is that you need to do in your life, write it down and start taking action right now! You're not getting any younger. You're not guaranteed another day. Start treating today as if it's the last day of your life. Start waking up earlier and go to bed later. Start eating healthier meals so you can lose weight, increase your energy, and start feeling like you did when you were in your twenties. Start your own business so you can be in control of your time and money.

Decide right now that you are no longer going to make excuses ever again. If you want to travel the world then do it right now! If you want to lose weight then do it right now! If you want to make more money do it right now! If you want to be happier then choose to be happier right now!

Stop being lazy! Stop complaining! Stop procrastinating! Stop feeling sorry for yourself! Stop saying you'll do it tomorrow! Enough is enough! The world doesn't care about your problems. They're only thinking about themselves.

Be the change you wish to see in the world. It must start with you. You have to be the one that changes. The only thing in the world that you can change is yourself. Doing nothing gets you nothing! It's time for you to start living the life of your wildest dreams. Don't wait another minute. Go out your front door early tomorrow morning and take back everything that belongs to you. Your life will never change until you stop making excuses and start taking action. There's no better time to start than right now! I wish you the best!

After you read this book would you mind doing me a huge favor please? Would you be kind enough to write me a five star customer review for this book on Amazon? By giving this book a good review it will help me as an author and help this book move up the rankings on Amazon. Your words have power. If you wouldn't mind supporting this book I would be extremely grateful. I would love to hear your feedback. You're welcome to contact me at me personal website anytime. If you would appreciate me sending you my self-publishing cheat sheet **ABSOLUTELY FREE**, just submit your name and email address at the link below. I wish you the very best of success in every area of your life!

Christopher Mitchell

www.ChangeYourLifeOvernight.com

If you enjoyed reading this book, here's more books by the author:

1. How To Lose Weight With Intermittent Fasting!

2. Sell Your First Book!

3. Money Meditation Manifestation!

4. My Inspiring True Life Story!

5. How To Get Rich From Home On A Part Time Basis With Only $20!

6. Why You're Fat & Sick And How To Fix It!

7. Vision Board Success!

8. How To Make Money As An Author Selling Your Books On Amazon!

9. Faith Produces Miracles!

All books can be purchased from:
www.amazon.com/author/fitchristophermitchell

www.ingramcontent.com/pod-product-compliance
Lightning Source LLC
Chambersburg PA
CBHW070103210526
45170CB00012B/732